Untangling the Knots

Untangling the Knots

Poems by

Buffy Aakaash

To Kathleen —
I'm so enjoying being in Otter
Creek Poets with you. Thanks
for your dedication to doing
good things ... and Untangling
the Knots!

♡ Buffy

Cover design by Shay Culligan
Cover art by Toni Austin-Allen

ISBN: 978-1-63980-227-2

Kelsay Books
502 South 1040 East, A-119
American Fork, Utah 84003
Kelsaybooks.com

I dedicate this book to the non-human beings who inspired me, particularly the plants, mountains, lands, and wildlife of New Mexico's El Morro Valley and Ancient Way (where I had the privilege to live on two separate occasions in my life). Also, the non-wild 4-leggeds who entered my life and at times helped make my life worth living and writing about.

Acknowledgments

I want to thank Maxima Kahn, poet, dancer, musician, and inspiration to creative impulses of everyone she meets, for her work in helping me fine-tune many of these poems. To Penny Hyde in New Mexico, for her close reading of this chapbook and the comments that helped me both with final edits and for the general shape and "volta" of the work. And to Zuni Mountain Poets. I appreciate their hearing me read many of these poems until we stopped meeting in person when the Covid pandemic began. Also thanks to Owl and Sunshine McCabe in Candy Kitchen, NM, who gave me a home, work, access to good food, and everything I needed to spend time doing what I love to do most.

Many thanks and appreciation to Toni Austin-Allen, who was inspired enough by this collection to create beautiful illustrations, one of which appears on the cover.

Finally, a big shout out and thank you to *Oberon Poetry Magazine* (www.OberonPoetry.com) for first publishing "How to Untangle a Knot" in 2007.

Oberon Poetry Magazine: "How to Untangle a Knot"

Contents

How to Untangle a Knot

Grasp a loose end in one hand
and in the other behold the heart of the matter.

Enter the entanglement
taking note the multitude of impetuous pathways.

Beware of free unravelings
entwining themselves into other snafus.

Pay no attention to seemingly unrelated cordage
encouraging resignation.

Ignore the growing turmoil
as you disengage snarls to enlarge the mass outward.

Refocus on the path
gently tugging loops that carry the loose end through the plight.

Repeat until fully unraveled.

Sort through the tethers.

Throw nothing away.

How to Be Real

There was a time when nothing,
not even tragedy, meant any end
to everything,
for we had each other
Not the facsimiles of you
those automated words
limited system phrases
that pretend to be you
but never approach the you I know

And I don't mean rather you in the flesh
because this is not about flesh
This is about the indescribable you
that lingers bewitching beneath the skin
and whispers after you're gone saying
Here I am in glorious imperfection
my foibles and indulgent incantations
Here I am take me or leave me as I am
without question unlike any other

But with labored reciprocities we direct
our gaze toward the bull-horning that proclaims
our presence when we are not
Nothing accounts for your likeness beyond words,
so frightening the life force in your bones
this auspicious delight of such beauty

Even the pure ingenuity of repulsion
which helps us to grow as we see
in ourselves what we hate so much

In all heartbreak we had each other
Not a disembodied voice or haphazard
arrangement of words meant to suffice.

How to Win

If we could thwart the cascade of projected losses
navigating exit polls that drop like cats & dogs
into currents of rage, our ultimate undoing,
careening over voluminous Falls from Grace

Having avoided the river swollen
from such unnatural outpourings

If we could loudly speak clean from within
our heart truth arising from that place far from
the republic's domain, that perch of the ballot box
shrouded in the democracy of opinions

we could shatter the history of delusions
that leave our Arcadian intentions
reeking in a heap of alternative facts

We could inspire a new world of brilliance
to breathe life into the wheezing metropolis
of the great forgotten ones:

the waters and the trees and all
the living body and soul we cannot lose
without our own untimely demise

Then might we discover this true victory
And safely lose ourselves for a time in this parade.

Rejoice!

How to Start a Fire

Gather some paper.
Preferably the headlines
of your life now at rest
in the news of the past.
Crumple it into balls
loose enough to catch a draft.
Place the small sticks,
each of those seasoned memories,
over the top.
And strike the match.

Now hear . . .
your needless worries incinerate
the conflagration of your worst fears
dancing in the burning wood.
Feel your heart.
How it inspires your love.
Smell the sweet alchemy
of your anger burnt away.
Place upon this growing passion
the next bigger log.

And continue to listen.

How to Pet a Cat

In loneliness
you already feel the longing
before this object of so many affections
appears with caution in his eyes.
You know the stronger hunger
giving birth to these encounters.
The mutual and primal desires
moving you both toward
necessary fettered entanglement.
But first you must look straight
through each other sensing the love
in the appreciation of time.

Then running your fingers
head to tail eliciting mutual
murmurings and silky growls
sparks flying from your fingers
in recognition of the pure sympathy
in the eyes of it all—
this shared life
this bundle of soft joy
before you in this quick
moment of gratitude.

How to Walk with a Puppy

A long-eared innocence will test your short
patience, your shame left at the door
as you barge out over tufts of grass
toward the trees below the ridges.

Immediately rapt with attention to details of your life
somewhere else you disengage.

      He stops and looks at you, head tilting left and right.
Sensing you. Questioning your innate distrust of idleness.

The canyon calls. You struggle over a fallen tree.

He knows his way around obstacles
in a way you wish to have learned sooner
Have you yet? Do you know if you must walk alone a while
your companion will join you on the path just
beyond this hurdle?   (I'm not sure I do.)

You've sidetracked again, you think. But what of it? he says.

He climbs up a sandy slope and slides down
over and over just for fun while your numb
sense of self warms with laughter.

Coming down off the canyon top to even
ground he takes off exuberant smiling
ears flapping across the open wide divide

as if there were nothing else in the world that matters.

Through his boisterous joy you divine true freedom
stopping time with mutual affection at play and slowing
down, grateful for how he raises you up

so that you may carry on.

How to Milk a Goat

She knows where you stand
In proximity to the box
Where she awaits
The scooping of
Scrumptious morsels
More pivotal than
Your crude fondling of her
Sacredness,

Which she holds close.
Her body in the cold
Contracting pouches of
Treasures embodied by
This particular life
We are akin to in ways
Beyond our immediate
Senses,

Which explode in perplexity.
Our touch evoking gripping unease
Disregarding our gentility
As if we could never quite live up
To the reality of her preciousness
And indeed perhaps are ignorant
Of her true nature as provider of
Life,

Which moves firmly onward.
She knows we will raise her offspring
To feed the people in exchange
Of disturbing and uncertain delight
For she acknowledges the horrors
Of separation as she stands beside us
In generosity with her life
Blood.

How to Undress

First begin by removing
all you've worn
from the moment
you pulled yourself from bed
dreading your world
as it breaks apart
from all your undoing.
Everyday wearing
the grief of your own
unravelling.
At the end of it all
button by button
you unfasten all the
mistakes
all the effrontery
the rudenesses endured
by ourselves or others.

To fully accomplish this
we simply set ourselves free
from whatever reduces mobility,
removing what has
imprisoned our waists
bound tightly our legs
or constricted our chests.
With each release
we throw down this life
we did not choose.
And then perhaps
and only then
we sink deep
into baffling prostration.
Or perhaps we lie back
our knees buckling
in passionate naked embrace
of ourselves or others.

We make love.
Our dreams
of some other life
bringing us to slumber

Then button by button
the next morning
we remember that joy
in shedding what holds
back our succession
so that we may
make it through
yet one more day
this travesty.

This is how it is done.

How to Follow a Path

If you were a wild spirit
horse trapped in a pen,
then suddenly set free,
where would you run?

You see no trails, no roads.
So you make your own retreat
through quick forays into
forbidden places.

You take pride in knowing
you alone have forged this
journey and it belongs to no
one but yourself.

But you loop back
to the same place
each time, nothing gained.

Then you see others
walking ancient paths
worn thousands of years,
passageways to places

few have been.
And you think how you've
been creating your wheels
as if they were new

but that turning's been done before.
So you join them and walk.
A path to follow not to make.
You pray to Spirit:

"Put me to work!"
And off you go, guided to
doorways you never knew existed.

In deference to unwavering
loyalty your commitment
to wisdom leads you to a
deep place in the woods

where the once blazed trail
has been brushed   over.
Snow,   rain,   wind,   sand.
Your way forward

                    obliterated,

and behind, the road you've walked
nothing but a   faint   scratch
in the earth   beckoning you
to lose   yourself   in   the journey
                          back.

How to Start Over

Sometimes the lights
go out. The stars you were following
now immersed in hopeless darkness.

When love died at the hands
of some formidable presence
I dug in my heels and wailed to no avail.

As those memories implode
in the fallows of Now I see
good fortune poisoned in the pains of the past.

From the ends of everything,
when they truly come, can the good
plant seeds of something new?

To have loved
may indeed be a seed for a life worth living.
But such platitudes do not instruct

how to let go
how to start over
with not a spark of imagination.

It has been said
the depth of love is
measured by the magnitude of grief.

I have loved deeply
then this life. For the earth moved
under my feet when the winds bore the clouds

and that star I watched
closely faded to dark bringing
not the end but new uprisings, a revolution.

My heart ruptures its defenses
opening a crack in the sidewalk and there
along the gray boulevard of despair bursts the purple iris.

How to Look at the Stars

Remember how very small we are
Crouched on the edge of night
When the home of these distant beings
throws open its pearly gates for all to see.
The last of the sun's light,

a creak of the hinges,
opening wide, wide open, so wide
it's hard not to resist what pulls
you up and away out of yourself.
For I've heard we are stardust

million-year-old karma
and the night sky our garden
in which we grow our dreams
from seeds of wishes
we never knew we made.

And look how our lives shower down
from a single shooting comet
whose tail disperses
light in dark matters
helping us to grow up

from where the seeds were planted
like the aftermath of
our great Daystar
which calls from the earth
the verdant lushness we know as home.

So too our home is in the stars
and while tiny enwrapped in it all,
so large our souls
we can barely keep our
feet on the ground.

How to Grow a Garden

First of all
begin with flowers
They will become the fruits
of all your endeavors

And when the hunger comes
you will have prepared
a field to sow the slow
recovery from perennial starvations.

When it comes time to plough
tread lightly the shallow soil for
your seeds will need the awareness
of the forest's delicate circuitry

as we too reach down through dark
fertility and climb up these
dismal vines of separation
our roots one day proving

true velocities through
space and time feeding
our deep breathing down
verdant rows of growing ancestors.

We have done this before
many times and we can
do it again now as
we await the great ripening.

How to Harvest Currants

Rest your weary back.
Treat yourself to plushness from
which to witness the sublime delectation
awaiting your earthly palate.

For you will not be reaching up
but rather bending down
to face the tiny fertile mysteries in
darkness swimming like the stars above.

You may find yourself here knee deep
many days bridging earth and sky
as waves of shiny black bundles
expose, ripen and unfold. Each time

pluck gently ensconced in nature and
tasting these sun-sweetened morsels
decipher the most divine ones dripping
with sugars released through perfect union.

Bite down on bitter tongues this day
and allow the depths of your heart
to root in the dark breaking new ground
for you this miracle of post-blossoming.

Thereby discover secrets of sweetness
the fruits of ripening gratitude
receiving this prayer with open hands
these gifts as humbly offered.

How to See a Flower

You behold beauty
and follow the call
without a thought

But you think
a flower just a flower
an object for desire

an expression of love
a symbol of living
And in this separation

your inner blossoming stops.

Remember majesty this
humous soil of humanity
unseen without your gaze

and step into your own
uniting the juxtaposed
melding love between you

Bringing together wildly
loose ends weaving
in reveling colors teeming

you deeply honor the elders.

Rocky soil beneath you
bathing in the sky
waters of journeys

grounding you forth
and engaging your gears
withheld by otherworldly

ones all around
gripping imaginations
of passersby who might

otherwise never know you.

How to Take a Hike

Ask yourself:

Will there ever be a day better
than this with the heavy
wind breaking your back
thunderheads ripe with
threats you feel in your
feet traversing a dry cracked
uneven ankle-torquing ground
that reminds you of
where you
stand
only you don't take
a stand this day
moving along you
boldly climb up and away
the nearest ridge
just in time for a light
rain but still clear
enough to see
where you just came
and how far
all these years
crossing a northern
flank the smell
of pine pitch the smell of
rain on dry ground the rustle
of oak leaves you confuse
with the rattle snaking a way
through this its own
world
letting thoughts shed
their skins and drop away
like the dead needles
you notice against

your soles when
the terrain changes
and you're moving
up the channels that will flash
flood with the help of
clouds
but yes the clouds
are levitating into ethers now
into celestial rivers of similes
we cannot like see but like feel
in that lightness of head
like those thoughts
trying to stick on you like
feathers to tar which
like in the hot sun
quickly
like melts away
and yes beyond
that mountain
peeks
a
blue
sky
hue
you've
never
seen
before?

And what was I
like thinking?

How to Climb a Mountain

No mountain is just a mountain.

Remember that as you chart your plan
to achieve the greatness of heights
never before reached.

Remember an exit strategy could be advisable
for when the legs begin to wobble
and the narrowed air

brings you to your knees shouting at the sky
for help with this untenable task you have
brought upon yourself engaging

with maybe not so much more than a molehill in the mind's eye
or a sacred tree, a holy altar so earthbound
you could miss it at first.

Never underestimate the immensity of those
seemingly small ventures that engage
your deep calling.

The intrigue of such endeavors can obscure
the enormity of these undertakings
beyond the veil.

Take strength and courage with you to know
what lies ahead or when to turn around
or when to attempt your solo ascent.

Your highest achievement may not be the summit
but in the end your immersion in the Ocean
where it all began.

How to Swim in the Ocean

Countless times
we wake up earlier
than desired fixating
on thorny transgressions:
who we have hurt
moving ahead ourselves
at the expense of others

We cross this jungle
and arrive at the beach
the waves of regret
vanquished by the rhythm
of the Great Mother
by her own rising up
and settling down

Over and over
uncoiling her deft fingers
against the solid ground
of immovable obligations
across this great divide
standing or swimming
running or rowing

Suddenly as at birth
naked infants we are
saltwater and sand pressed
wet between our fledgling toes
sea-misted breeze
glazing our cheeks
emblazoned with gratitude

She cannot grant us absolution.
But she invites our needed rest
against her fiercely soft swells
never letting us forget her
capacities unparalleled in potency
and her propensity for tenderness
amidst this mammoth turbulence

At her bidding we release our resistance
take in heart the aromas of fresh death
reborn in the sanctity of her salty breath
and cross an unmapped threshold
commencing into her inscrutable love.

How to Plunge into a River
(in Two Steps)

1. You consider this moment

Standing on the rock
Hearing the shrieking
the splashes below
the bodies shrinking in
icy waters gushing

with resolve you make your entrance
for which there is a before
and there is an after.

Something magical charges the in-between

with the arrival of

Silence

when

your life rhythm

     stops

caught between your past
as melting snow and
your future in the belly
of a vast and
salty womb.

2. You rise to the occasion

Break the surface
remember to breathe
grasp your heart
in the clasp of your
desperate hand

Your feet
one then the other
find rounded slippery stones
clawing the flood bank
dropping back into the sun
embracing again warm ground

Trees sighing overhead
river rushing
returning time
to its bounds
you wonder what
just transpired

And then this happens.
And then this happens.
And then this happens.

How to Die

My father left behind so many miracles:

sun dappling the wall in the afternoon
breeze blowing through an open window.

We held hands, hearts in sync, ancestral kinship peering
through his mother's eyes and straight through mine

striving to sail first across the finish line
this humble gamesmanship his only diversion

from a life graciously arranged through time
a plotting of loving deeds done in earnest.

His Quaker roots planted deep this divine
equanimity gently guiding rarely demanding

branches bursting with flowering treasures
the good children he knew we were and would be.

In our final moments: he worried I would die young
in that last great pandemic he watched claim my brother.

With a glance through the window he took in that sun
wind rustling the trees, and at last he knew he could

let me go.

    And I him.

How to Stay Alive

Beware of your fear striving to keep you alive
amidst all these unfounded threats.

The fighter jets that will target your car as you
race across familiar roads now forbidden

under lockdowns and curfews meant to prevent
the spread of those mysterious diseases.

We bring this upon ourselves through disregard
this failing faltering and falling

with no vaccine for such things.

Embrace instead the sick and dying
in your heart share your mother spirit

with those struggling to breathe
under duress of forces over which we have no control

seek refuge in kindness toward those
we barely comprehend outside the bounds of our longing

for some vestige of justice beyond the righteous
heads shaking in disbelief over the improbable news.

Here is our vaccination:

acknowledge our estranged roots in the soil
of our ancestors nourishing our every move

out beyond ourselves in brittle stillness
winter into spring racing for the sky

forging our way around the old solid things
that block our path to summer's brightenings:

darkened canopies of hardwood or the wheeze of cicadas
against the evergreens blistering in the emboldening sun

giving way that awakening to the autumn reminders
that forces at work without likewise play within

then like the trees something of us will remain alive.

About the Author

Buffy Aakaash grew up around hills and lakes in New Jersey west of New York City. He has lived as a queer man in both big cities—New York, Seattle, San Francisco—and small remote towns throughout the US. His work has been published by *Vultures & Doves, Sweety Cat Press, The Write Launch, Main Street Rag, New Feathers Anthology, Dissonance Magazine,* and others. Currently, he lives with his dog, Bodhi, in the Green Mountains of Vermont, growing and supporting community there. His published work can be seen at BuffyAakaashPoetry.com.